SKIN

SKIN

TYLER PENNOCK

Brick Books
Prince Edward County, Ontario

Library and Archives Canada Cataloguing in Publication
Title: Skin / Tyler Pennock.
Names: Pennock, Tyler, 1977- author
Identifiers: Canadiana (print) 20260188247 | Canadiana (ebook) 20260188271 | ISBN 9781771316767 (softcover) | ISBN 9781771316781 (PDF) | ISBN 9781771316774 (EPUB)
Subjects: LCGFT: Poetry.
Classification: LCC PS8631.E567 S55 2026 | DDC C811/.6—dc23

We gratefully acknowledge the Canada Council for the Arts, the Government of Canada through the Canada Book Fund, the Ontario Arts Council, and the Government of Ontario for their support of our publishing program.

Canada Council for the Arts Conseil des arts du Canada Canada ONTARIO ARTS COUNCIL CONSEIL DES ARTS DE L'ONTARIO an Ontario government agency un organisme du gouvernement de l'Ontario Ontario

Edited by Dallas Hunt.
Author photo by Michael David White.
The book is set in Minion Pro.
Cover by Ovila Mailhot.
Design by Marijke Friesen.

Brick Books
www.brickbooks.ca

BRICK BOOKS poetry's home

CERTIFIED CANADIAN PUBLISHER

Though much of the work of Brick Books takes place on the ancestral lands of the Anishinaabeg, Haudenosaunee, Huron-Wendat, and Mississaugas of the Credit peoples, our editors, authors, and readers from many backgrounds are situated from coast to coast to coast in Canada on the traditional and unceded territories of over six hundred nations who have cared for Turtle Island from time immemorial. While living and working on these lands, we are committed to hearing and returning the rightful imaginative space to the poetries, songs, and stories that have been untold, under-told, wrongly told, and suppressed through colonization.

IN MEMORY OF
THE
NATIVE PEOPLE
AND THE
EARLY SETTLERS
BURIED IN THE
SAWRIDGE
CEMETERY

— *Township Rd 731C, Slave Lake*

Praise for *Skin*

"What if home is a cemetery erased by floods, where so many layers of erasure have taken place that it is nearly impossible to speak of oneself or of one's community? Tyler Pennock invents a language in which to do so, one made of rapid, defamiliarized English and a newly re-acquired Cree, a language of blueberries in the freezer, crushed cigarette butts in a coffee cup, kittens appearing unexpectedly beneath a trailer porch. This is a book of looking through skin, of returning on a radically shifted topography, of love and of rage all residing together to reconstruct a livable home beneath which the dead still remember the coming generations."

— Larissa Lai, author of *The Lost Century*

"The poetry in Tyler Pennock's *Skin* unfurls through such delicate observances: 'imagine an opening / an outward push / an expansion down a route / a spread in the trees.' Layered with a gentle melody, Pennock writes each line with an attentive breath, thoughtfully attuned to the quietness of being. *Skin* is a collection that understands how 'every utterance / is a drop pulled / from a puddle / evaporating,' reminding us to pay attention to what is nearly gone, and what has always quietly existed."

— David Ly, author of *Mythical Man*

Praise for *Bones* and *Blood*

"Pennock's shifting, expansive book-length poem luminously reflects the scattered fragments of memory with language that fluidly mixes abstraction, reflection and recurrent imagery. *Bones* gradually unveils the pain and trauma that seeps through time and relations, in a way that mimics the heart's unveiling of itself. His touchstones of Indigenous ceremony and ritual ground the collection in a way that navigates the reader through a rich archaeology of bones that are not merely relics, but oracles."

— Jury Citation, 2021 Gerald Lampert Memorial Award

"Lyrical, witty, heart-wrenching, and empowering, Pennock's debut book of poetry is a contemplative epic asking us to ponder the ethics of remembrance in all of its lacings of razing and revitalization."

— Joshua Whitehead, author of *Full-Metal Indigiqueer*

"Here is a spare and urgent voice that speaks of 'wounds and beauty,' that gestures to a story of trauma and abuse while offering us a potent journey of self-reckoning and reclamation. *Bones* entwines brutality with the deepest tenderness and in its clear-eyed way asks us, as poetry must, to re-see the world."

— Catherine Bush, author of *Blaze Island*

"Tyler Pennock's poetry unfurls like breath: measured, light, caught, whispering, and vital. It charts memory with a steady hand and unerring allegiance to locating the 'beauty/in terrible things.' *Bones* addresses the effects of intergenerational, state-sponsored trauma with an enviable grace, inscribing and affirming life on the other side of overwhelming pain, abuse, and grief. It carries on, resilient, defiant, gazing at the stars, one breath at a time."

— Laurie D. Graham, author of *Fast Commute*

"The poems in Tyler Pennock's *Blood* generate a gentle music that is in turns both painful and reverent (sometimes at the same time). I value the way Pennock sits with contradiction and in doing so makes a whole spectrum of feeling possible. An important addition to a blossoming queer Indigenous literary tradition."

— Billy-Ray Belcourt, author of *A Minor Chorus*

"Pennock's *Blood* shines on the parts of the self that defy the ruthlessness of empire. By turns inward to the still and sobering power of language, and again outward to the echoes of 'leaves and wind,' a music as sensitive as it is revelatory ushers us into their unique measure of aliveness. The poet here is engaged and unafraid to look long."

— Canisia Lubrin, author of *The Dyzgraphxst*

Intimacy isn't a definite, discrete thing – it is a pattern

an instinct

as unique to the weaver

as the place they occupy –

Slightly wet
and wisping
the knitted ends
of a spider's
sheet silk
float in the
warming air
                    a
          carpet woven
                    a
repetition interlaced
compounding trails

their lightness against the grass
the fingerprint of past bearings
a mirrored beacon, a spider's darkroom
          efflorescence for direction

billowing in the charged air
to catch a branch
          a breeze
untethered by morning

and spider's enduring skill
          for weaving

Fourteen thousand threads
twist, contort, and
bind
Some fibres
pull, others
braid and bunch
attracting each other
opening
cavities dry
for moisture
lain and layered –

graphite tears from a pencil tip
carbon over carbon
rolling across a desk
in front of a child's silhouette
their pencil's reduction
losing against filaments crossed
finely
tells of removal
distance
and hope

where angled scratches on

Paper

speak of evergreens
against a late evening sunset
that hide an imagined town
lowering
just ahead of a falling sun

Home Is the smell of black and white spruce in a late August sunset home is an early morning wind through swaying trees home is burnt trunks and branches years old viewed through a bus window home is a souterrain house long forgotten in the hills behind a Walmart home is a homestead fallen behind grass and feed home is a cemetery erased by floods home is gravestones overturned and sunken home is dozens of mason jars lined up by a stove in July home is blueberries across the lake home is blueberries in freezer bags home is crushed and bent cigarette butts in a coffee cup under a canopy held down by steel wheels home is hands rooting through dirt for potatoes home is coyotes playing outside a horse farm at night home is a contracting barn roof scaring your nephew at night home is a childless mother calling her cat in starlight home is a litter of kittens appearing unexpectedly under a trailer porch home is a long dirt road from the highway to the lake home is a circle of Elders' homes with no Elders in them home is a charred hotel at the side of the road home is a misplaced diary home is a river home is a river split and emptied into marsh home is grass encroaching on a wooded lake home is pencil scratches standing in for the smell of black and white spruce home is home is a memory of trees you've never seen home is Muksim's house built into the hill home is a road leading into the woods on the hill behind the Walmart home is a marriage record from 1917 home is learning your first Cree word home is learning any word that isn't in English home is a rolling carbon graphite point scribbling relatives down as fast as your Uncle can say them home is a pattern revealed your children home is a chipmunk darting behind a sleeping dog home is eight white geese scaring off predators home is a garden home is a garden in your uncle's home is the memory of your grandmother's

garden home is stories about bears shared over cigarettes
under a canopy in the yard while geese listen home is Walmart
running out of mason jars in July home is stories of a vicious
cane-wielding Chiâpan home is an entire community walking
a body to the RCMP while an angry bear stalks them home
is the lines a boy follows on the way to his relatives' houses
home is a story told in trusted company home is the memories
that extend beyond church pictures home is a carpet woven by
movement home is a confluence of stories that continue home
is **a Low Hum** home is tributary home is a lake home is rainfall
drumming on a brown trailer in canyon creek in summer
home is a nephew frightened by the noises a barn makes in the
cooling summer evening home is the dogs that sleep through
the noises a barn makes but howl when they hear a scared
nephew pacing home is the curiosity of horses when a nephew
visits home is stories told from a kitchen in August home is
the way a family forgets beauty in terrible things home is the
way roots find space in soil home is where they used to hang
fish home is a lake that spawns slow meandering rivers home
is where the waters collect before **Dispersing** home is a place
we used to gather home is all these things as rivers and creeks
scatter a lake's body home is never a starting point

SAWRIDGE

A
sign stands
languid
over leaning grass
while the
wind soothes
aeolian over bodies
earth-cradled and fading
under a burst of mayflies

Wooden crosses
painted without names
angle slowly
        seeking respite

Individuating memories
is too much
for whitened wood
in flooded fields sieved
        by chain-link fences

Should I become a memory, they say
                                                  think of me
as permeable
a silhouette, colours liquid
bright and congested

Should I become a history, they say
                                                  imagine for me
I am metastasizing
words testing a cradle unravelling

Should I become a story, they say
                                                  describe for me
that it is stubborn, where letters stray from their words
tangling, listener and teller coiled
          penned in percolation

Should I become a footnote, they say
                                                  listen for me
where my inclusion is a wound
blood fills the inadequacies
of today, and two bodies are paragraphs
leaking letters to fill an invisible third

Should I become darkness, they say
                                                  hope with me
that it is reflexive
light turning a swollen quiet, a tract
mourning its own creation

Should I become an

Epigraph

stay with me
hold my words

gently
they say
they say

When did home become
  a connection
          only traced on paper

kiiwe giiwe kîwew giiwe kîwew kîwew kîwew kîwew kîwew giiwe
kîwew kîwew kîwew giiwe kîwew kiiwe kîwew kîwew kîwew
kîwew kîwew kîwew kîwew kiiwe kîwew kiiwe kîwew kîwew
kîwew giiwe kîwew kîwew kîwew kîwew kiiwe kîwew kîwew
kîwew kîwew kîwew kiiwe kîwew kîwew kîwew kîwew kîwew
kîwew giiwe kîwew kîwew giiwe kîwew kîwew kiiwe kîwew
kîwew kîwew kîwew giiwe kîwew kîwew kiiwe kîwew giiwe
A teacher, friend
kîwew kîwew kîwew kîwew kiiwe kîwew kîwew giiwe kîwew
once told me
kîwew kîwew kîwew kîwew kiiwe kîwew kîwew kiiwe kîwew
that a pipe
kîwew kiiwe kîwew kiiwe giiwe kîwew giiwe kîwew kîwew
or drum
kîwew kîwew kîwew giiwe kîwew kîwew kîwew giiwe kîwew
is a tool
kiiwe kîwew kîwew kîwew kîwew kîwew kîwew kîwew kiiwe
kîwew kiiwe kîwew kîwew kîwew giiwe kîwew kîwew kîwew
that I should always look
kîwew kiiwe kîwew kîwew kîwew kîwew kîwew kiiwe kîwew
through
kîwew kîwew kîwew kîwew kîwew giiwe kîwew kîwew giiwe
kîwew kîwew kiiwe kîwew kiiwe kîwew kîwew kîwew giiwe
There I was
kîwew kîwew kiiwe kîwew giiwe kîwew kiiwe kîwew kîwew
trying to discern
kîwew kiiwe kîwew kîwew giiwe kîwew kîwew kîwew kîwew
patterns of thickness
kîwew kiiwe kîwew kîwew kiiwe kîwew kîwew kiiwe kîwew
in the hide
kiiwe giiwe kîwew giiwe kîwew kîwew kîwew kîwew kîwew
giiwe kîwew kîwew kîwew giiwe kîwew kiiwe kîwew kîwew
Grinning, he said
kîwew kîwew kîwew kîwew kiiwe kîwew kiiwe kîwew kiiwe
it was a start
kîwew kîwew kîwew giiwe kîwew kîwew kîwew kîwew kiiwe
kîwew kîwew kîwew kîwew kîwew kiiwe kîwew kîwew kîwew
kîwew kîwew kîwew giiwe kîwew kîwew giiwe kîwew kîwew
kiiwe kiiwe kîwew kîwew kîwew kîwew giiwe kîwew kîwew
kiiwe kîwew giiwe kîwew kîwew kîwew kîwew kiiwe kîwew
kiiwe kîwew giiwe kîwew kîwew kîwew kiiwe kîwew kîwew
kiiwe kîwew kîwew kiiwe kîwew kîwew kiiwe kîwew kîwew
kiiwe kîwew kîwew kîwew kîwew kîwew kîwew kiiwe kîwew
kiiwe kîwew kiiwe kîwew kîwew kîwew giiwe kîwew kîwew

Birdsong

We
call

beautiful
without
knowing the
    message
criss-crossing
through
trees
its tenor trespassing
audience and
melodist
alike
    thoughts
transmuted by
air density and
electrical charge
carried
over breezes and
foliage
    caught –
recognized through bodies
cast in melody
hardened in song

    this lyric
incomprehensibility
repudiating
the scant
    words

we create
to describe
them

Some stories lean hard into their listener
a bloodless hand-mark radiating
while colour hesitates

Others are gentle
cycling over wind gusts
and car engines
coaxing an ear softly

Others, lighter still
are memories without image
an absence unstudied
– petrified roots
high on a canyon slope

If you wore your stories
could a listener discern the weaver of every line?
The tool that tore every depression
in its rolling wake?

If every story told was birdsong
what scars would
the wind carry away with it?

Would the lightness
of repeated injury
stain the sky?

Victims' screams
in horror movies
through stark orchestral strings
announce injury
as though a wound
a shriek
or blood's escape
needed
amplification and
exposed
bones and
tissue
weren't warning
enough
to avoid
the curiosity
of a pressed
blade
Or maybe
we are meant to
believe
the air is caustic and
vulnerable places are embodied revulsion
awaiting release
that nothing should exist
outside its boundary
that **Fences, Walls** are
pain's benefit to be loved
as though we grew them ourselves

I lie in a field, and there are scores of others lying with me – in waving, crossing, branching lines, like children's unpatterned escapes from a schoolroom's discipline every afternoon; the sun's warmth declaring it's time instead to be driven by natural things . . . things like home.

We grow long, into lines, until we're joined, piled, knitted, and crossing – like the grasses we lie in. Meanwhile, the sun's reddening coaxes each of us to grow over each other in chaos, without complaint, until tightly knotted.

Some of us grow into a dandelion stalk, some stretch to alter the flower's direction – lengthening to help the whole. Ensuring the sun doesn't glut parts already sated. As I pull away, I see a continent of people patterned like this, fierce, supportive, and free, the spaces between us shrinking.

I feel like a safety deposit **Box**
bolts and combinations
announcing that someone owns
the valuables I've kept

but
left alone so long
that there's no
one living
to claim
them

Adoption is just a

Word

that veils a shape-softening barrier replacing true things such as touch warmth and detail with paper-thin distances or scrims meant for shadows and filling the unknowns with whatever your mind can muster instead of a knowing darkness on which we can scratch our internal difference so the light can enter like the way prisms force trillions of reflections refractions each stealing energy until the whole can't be perceived and then you'd think silence and darkness our undisturbed natural state on which any meaning can be written future authors not knowing the strength of previous harms and how their atrophy leaks warmth to be remembered leaves darkened scars to remind us this skin is like dry riverbeds its depressions a history of how our bodies gave way for thirst

I wish I could reach the people who conceived this policy movement, to see how they considered its violent nature and decided that its purpose was reason enough, to know how they grant the wounds formed of its careless, thrashing intervention – but words are all I have

print words saved words protected words inviolable words weighted words with the holding force of a singularity words binding heft words just shy of love words meant to sublimate words – with cracks in them

only a child can notice

Words a mother saves for her child that no one hears, words a child strains to hear in every interaction, soils beckoning water that can't repair, that merely deepens what was taken

A water droplet
thick and full
trails pieces
of itself
down the long plane
of a dandelion stalk

loosing itself
fumbling its body
to tiny viridescent incursions –

a vertical landscape
green and vicious
tears into a curved image
compressed
          tighter
with every slip
downward toward the earth
parched
by the **Dandelion's Thirst**

I fear that
on paper
coming home
implies a return
along the same
narrow path
that I left

that reclamation
is a retracing
walking face down and
forward
while

Ghosts,
Poised

grin in the trees

that my return is
narrowed by a path
you already know
well

Fuck returning
seriously

In your hands
home's image
is steel-brushed
and fogged

in your memory

Kîwew

Returning

is a topography
shifted
by our lack of
shared
context

and every utterance
is a drop pulled
from a puddle
evaporating

Father, S*n

I wonder
how the texture
of my woolen memories might disrupt
your calico hues
        whether this unkempt
        experience sheared by
        anger, abuse
        and unfinished loneliness
is meaningful
        visible to you
or if you'd shy
from my fleecy story
        carded over pitted
memories and disproportionate love
with colours unevenly spun
        like the rutted brown
        joy in Kyle's
        eyes, grinning
                as he dances
        over our
        early sunlight-washed
chestnut linoleum floor

I wonder how your linen
patterns wrinkle
in the late afternoon wind
or if the bioaccumulation
        of jagged detergent-silences
has smoothed over your
own disorganized fringes

your riot fading
recklessly

I hope still the reddening darkness
of each sunset over our silence
our pitched remnants
the offcut and shredded rags
of our carved relationship
bear a scarlet signal
you might
one day
recognize

This is not a memoir
unless we agree
no remembering is
        ever about the self

This is not a memory
unless we understand
them as the hopes
of failing dreams
        that clutch at stars
saving enough daylight
to remember

This is not a story
unless we see
        that no day bears
the fullness of sunlight
        unfiltered

Is it a dream, then?
And if so
are we all not failed stars
        storying our bravado
as our unfinished pieces
hurtle through darkness?

Uncle Remi,

if memory is a purchase
of futures imagined
squarely in the past
is story then a wave?
A shudder in the self
squeezing and stretching
impossibly fast?
A clasping and craning
the recurrent novae of
our family's seasonal
destruction felt as a quiver
owned and then embodied
myopia woven
in the attraction
between bodies, imperceptible?
What then

up
out
over

are the dreams
and constraints
that ripple
through us?

I think I've lost something
in the late angle of the sunlight
peeking through curtains unravelling
and a dozen pacing dogs
under the sound of Uncle Remi's
          steady breathing
over pictures scattered
          in pause
as if old photos
were asking for threads
to tie them finally
          together

Yes, something's gone

in the comfort of this moment
in the memory of Uncle Muksim's
          subterranean house
          on a hillside removed
          for a parking lot
in the horses outside
in the chaos of dogs
in the late-night coyote calls
and the barn roof that
          pops and groans
imitating an old man's shuffle

in a long sunset that needs
no remembering

in the recorded stories

and pictures I'll likely

        never need to
revisit

Untitled

All the words
I've kept

dreamed, forged
and forgotten
unaspirated
return seeping
as exudate reversed
revoked
rescinded
recalled, reserved

words left for greater
personal relevance
all molten once
lie now as
blooms, billets
and hammer scale
fired and cooled
registered
recorded
rostered
kept
Words I've forged
and forgotten
later dreamed
are insufficient
to recount
the torments lived
by any of us

in subjection

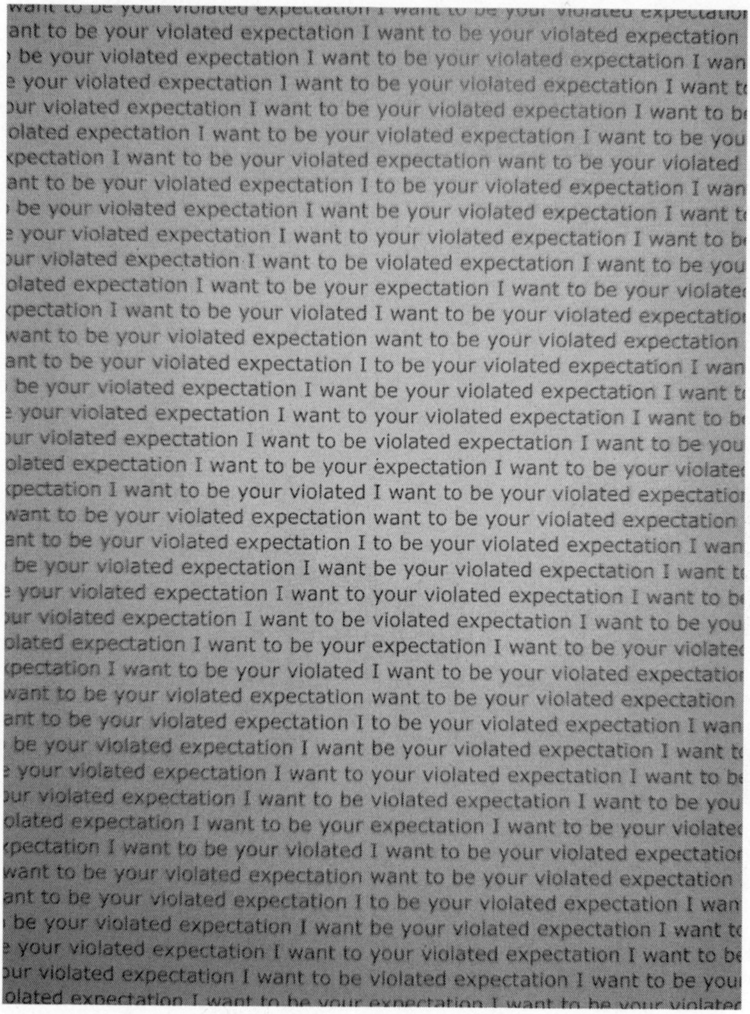
ant to be your violated expectation I want to be your violated expectation
be your violated expectation I want to be your violated expectation I wan
your violated expectation I want to be your violated expectation I want t
ur violated expectation I want to be your violated expectation I want to b
olated expectation I want to be your violated expectation I want to be you
xpectation I want to be your violated expectation want to be your violated
ant to be your violated expectation I to be your violated expectation I wan
be your violated expectation I want be your violated expectation I want t
your violated expectation I want to your violated expectation I want to b
ur violated expectation I want to be violated expectation I want to be you
olated expectation I want to be your expectation I want to be your violate
xpectation I want to be your violated I want to be your violated expectatio
want to be your violated expectation want to be your violated expectation
ant to be your violated expectation I to be your violated expectation I wan
be your violated expectation I want be your violated expectation I want t
your violated expectation I want to your violated expectation I want to b
ur violated expectation I want to be violated expectation I want to be you
olated expectation I want to be your expectation I want to be your violate
xpectation I want to be your violated I want to be your violated expectatio
want to be your violated expectation want to be your violated expectation
ant to be your violated expectation I to be your violated expectation I wan
be your violated expectation I want be your violated expectation I want t
your violated expectation I want to your violated expectation I want to b
ur violated expectation I want to be violated expectation I want to be you
olated expectation I want to be your expectation I want to be your violate
xpectation I want to be your violated I want to be your violated expectatio
want to be your violated expectation want to be your violated expectation
ant to be your violated expectation I to be your violated expectation I wan
be your violated expectation I want be your violated expectation I want t
your violated expectation I want to your violated expectation I want to b
ur violated expectation I want to be violated expectation I want to be you

Untitled*

is my resistance
to definitive
    inferences
    intimations
that divorce essence
from the speaker
    or a silk that
    loses its spider
Untitled is
    an irritation
    a rile
to whoever encounters it
with no desire to know
the journey a thread tells

Untitled

are the white spaces
short lines
and scarcity

the places
I don't want
        to name

bring too much light on
        Undiverted glares
        grow features
too
        blanched, salted
        brine-crystallized
        and caustic

for abundance

One – two – three –

Seven – eight – nine – stop

Twenty-one- twenty-two- stop –

Count them out

Measure

forty.
forty-one.

stop.

the intervals

sixty.
sixty-one.
between one cricket call
stop.

and the next

see if it's true
if the loss is
noticeable

the widening emptiness

from butterflies to
dragonflies darting

between mosquitos

Tell me I'm wrong. Tell me that it's because I live in an urban area. Tell me I've always had to travel, ride thirty minutes out – before I'd see any. Tell me it's only happening here. Tell me they're just waiting –

like birds during bombings
measuring the silence
between mortar bursts
and whistling shells

stop.

Please

tell me it's not too late
and that this
our silence
isn't growing

Un titled

is a scapulimancy

a canon made
for living bodies
        features presented
        on new bones

interpretations fringed
by story, connection, kin
        and the events
that eddy underneath

If a word is a
form better held
by transcription
in stasis
                    hardened

then I prefer my cognitions destructible
          permeable silhouettes
liquids shaped by
          their own tension
          never static or contained
irreducible

Immobile substance
is an aberration
time and nuance
are an oxidation
and alterity
          is an equalizing force

All things are subject
to the impatience of
          their elements
and words deserve no
protection

          Paragraphs are
spontaneous cadavers
constitution is temporary
and meaning's solidification
is a desperate hope for futile ends

We're all in line, excited and loud, awaiting our turn on Canada's newest ride, the RESIDENTAL SCHOOLS APOLOGY. *We've received all the assurances of proper maintenance and repair, signs everywhere giving a sense of security. News reports and YouTube segments repeat that this ride will outlast them all, and never fail to time, weather, rust, or the self-importance and smug abandon of the ride's designers. Still, we see in the faces of park staff that they know the ride better than the riders do, barking orders and reading scripts at us. A small voice tells me maybe someone didn't check all the pieces, trusted too much in ingenuity. Then, before the start, I look down and see the ground below, waiting expectant like a soundless, wide-open mouth. Hand out, desperate for a scream or even just a word, anything to pause it, I'm seized by paralysis as my shoulders forget the feel of the ride guards, and I hold on, every muscle trembling, constricted, taut, knowing that my grip is slipping . . .*

then clarity, resignation, and futility unfold with the sound of morning birds and sunlight through my window, a familiar place where

words are
valued for their
emptiness

equity
is anathema

the law is an absent
partner that eats dinner and leaves

unseen while children's hunger
is a stomach that
eats itself

nationhood
is an anechoic chamber
intent astray in
a fractal void
and empire is thirty-nine million
        empty
        mirrors

This

Old Nightmare

is a void told by
unreverberant green drapes
its hushed, subdued, tranquilized
arrested
words, debates, commissions, policies
weep into tables
and carpeted stairs
a low hum of complacency

Impotence is the price of office
the badge of one's
learned helplessness

caveats and conventions
comprise a broken body
while underneath
corridors criss-cross ahead of a tower
a figure wrought in skin
without bone, nerve, and muscle
whose prominence
leaches

where willful, deliberate
ignorance is a rendering
subjection and constraint
are panoptic

telling you that if you hold out
against variation

long enough
ears clasped
eyes biting
hard against change, a tautology forms
blisters beneath the
skin, dark and pooling

grasping for more skin
to unseat

Properly unquenched
a good ignorance
can murmur
along under the skin
muting
compassion
concern
love
for
decades

A Purple Tiger Named Pope Joan Wears Zippered Sneakers Designed by Colby

Some of the boldest places have now fallen
to entropy and a form of queer
sealed by wedding rings
and preference for private acts

Maybe it was time
and not a change in us that
lead to their demise

If I'm wrong

I hope I'm not the only one
staring a little too long in doorways

at steps and
sidewalks
dominated by
banks and startup restaurants

I wonder if introducing titles
to my poetry may cause
people to read them
in the order they appear

but really, I'm more
interested in why
the absence of titles
encouraged random
page flipping

I'm
just the shape of a person
        no detail
except for what you imagine

Today
it's easy to settle with that
                    – which I mourn

Imaginings become reality
in spaces assumed empty

                            and

few dare to look
                            study
the nature of our
connection
        relation
to each other

__titled

is a disaggregate

unleashing distance
          capacity
where centred others
would force words, implications
carried across anarchic, hungry oceans
water trapped in repeating
recursive
recurring
recapitulatory
cycles

My aunts tell me
that I have relatives
buried in the original
Sawridge cemetery
but I'm scared to trust
        the petrifaction
        of bones mineralizing
        bodies hardened
        a leached record –
memory
is best as a storied
        event

Perhaps ghosts
are people without
                    title
beings, unassociated
their mode of
relation unrecognized
a reality unaspirated

motives drifting
through the air
        awaiting purchase

real, but
erased
by a growing
incomprehension
in the rest of us

As ghosts maybe
we can dance
until the air we kick
up is enough to tickle
this country into
remembering

Sâkahikan

A Lake

a hole in a map
a reservoir
a pond
a basin of water
currents held firm
by rock and dirt
seeping slower than the rain
precious for what it contains
and a stillness that rivers lack –

imagine an opening
an outward push
an expansion down a route
a spread in the trees
on a map, a place to swim
or leap

a collection of promontories
rounded by earth
chances to bridge
a chance to grow
stretch

like the air catching
spiders on extended webs

precious for how it expresses a change
in whatever encounters it

I remember listening to the second iteration of Joshua Whitehead's presentation "Queer Indigenous Futurisms: Stone & Slipstream," eyes closed and slightly grinning, listening for the growth and adaptation of his gorgeous text in a new space, loving the use of Anihshininiimowin, Anishinaapemowin, and Nehiyawewin with an abandon meant for revolution and wilful destruction of property, the kind of destruction that honours people over buildings and commodities, true value over owned value, a careful and caring expression of ideas meant for the here and now, the space we occupy, centred on the land where we sit, like a rabbit stew made not how you were taught, but a relational stew, with found parts from the current geography, not the remembered one –

love-words, that was the way I could describe them, his voice expressing a love for land, meeting places, different people, different languages, and the ways they interact, like a good meal, its scent inviting others to join

He shared that *kinoo* infers a kind of opening, an expanding, a spreading like a camera shutter, and I wanted to tell him that day
about a friend, Jake Kakegamic, telling me that
Kihkinoohamaakewin felt like pouring
water from one container to another
and then another, and another
which I felt was an
intergenerational
growth of
liquid bodies

I don't mean to suggest that language is a useful placebo for all our problems, but that many words require a connection, an experience to anchor themselves to

and Anishiniimowin taught me that means
there's almost always a
way to trace any word back home

Falling, I curled into myself, my body, my skin trying to slink away from itself, from the smash, from the impact of the ground below. Pieces of me were folding over other pieces, my skin growing ever tighter, expressing fault lines like a yarn ball pulled too tight. Everything in me was impossibly tight, my skin piled, knitted, and crossing from the stress. I was like a collapsing universe – tightly wrapped around a centre that was depleting. I screamed, but the scream shot out like a thread, my skin circling forward and inward to try and stop it.

On the line I kept leaving bits of myself – cells – the line picking up the shed filaments of what time would leave.

I realized then that the line I was weaving was a smaller version of all my experiences, storied. That my telling was moving through me, eastward. My voice was my remembering coagulated, a telling of my present for people in the future, whose present was my failed imagining.

The thread continued through me; as I fell behind, I continued to shrink, until I was barely a mote.

I could say I fear the ocean for how it can swallow beings whole. Cold density anticipating falling bodies like cortisol in a mind wrought by abuse.

I could say I abhor the wind for how it carries sound. Rounding, testing entropy in every direction but to you.

I could say I dislike the river for being unvarying in its will, reducing, lathing the earth without pause or consideration.

But for now, let's say anything

anything to describe the decay between friends, poets met in spaces briefly conjured between empires that hoped to silence them. Say, should we never again meet, it's enough to briefly speak against the harm in topographies that remain

terrifying

Don't do that
don't whistle
my friend, teacher
told me
not at night
not during the northern lights
but in a hospital

Later
after hearing countless
whistles in sweats
and shake tents
I discovered that

to invite relationship
without a common
interpretation

is like pouring water into a sieve
and telling someone to drink it

insisting they're no longer thirsty
while they gulp at cold air

When someone is consumed by the desire to consume a community is devoured fear becomes the person someone disappears obsession overtakes a life that birthed it strength becomes the person someone fades someone is effaced by their own creation someone takes until only they are left someone can't separate from their consuming something consumes itself nothing is left we have a name when someone is consumed by the desire to consume a community is devoured fear becomes the person someone disappears obsession overtakes a life that birthed it strength becomes the person someone fades someone is effaced by their own creation someone takes until only they are left someone can't separate from their consuming something consumes itself when nothing is left we have a name when someone is consumed by the desire to consume a community is devoured fear becomes the person someone disappears obsession overtakes a life that birthed it strength becomes the person someone fades someone is effaced by their own creation someone takes until only they are left someone can't separate from their consuming something consumes itself nothing is left we have a name when someone is consumed by the desire to consume a community is devoured when fear becomes the person someone disappears obsession overtakes a life that birthed it strength becomes the person someone fades someone is effaced by their own creation someone takes until only they are left someone can't separate from their consuming something consumes itself nothing is left we have a name when someone is consumed by the desire to consume a community is devoured fear becomes the person someone disappears obsession overtakes a life that birthed it strength becomes the person someone fades someone is effaced by their own creation someone takes until only they are left someone can't separate from their consuming something consumes itself nothing is left we have a name when someone is consumed by the desire to consume when a community is devoured fear becomes the person someone disappears when obsession overtakes a life that birthed it when strength becomes the person someone fades someone is effaced by their own creation someone takes until only they are left, someone can't separate from their consuming something consumes itself nothing is left we once a name when someone is consumed by the desire to consume when a community was devoured fear became the person someone disappeared when obsession overtook a life that birthed it when strength became the person someone faded someone was erased by their own creation someone took until only they were left, someone

people consumed by absence and lack but those were evacuated, subsumed by stories about werewolves and giants and **Thus, Imaginary**

If the turtle was stolen
and we were all
earth in a muskrat's
clenched paw

what
would we use
to hold us

all

together?

Reluctant Superheroes

In the post-therapy glow of our twelfth week
together I called our chat group the
Tuesday OCD
                    Stark Banality was our name
because I couldn't spare the
time
        I couldn't create a fitting set of
sounds to capture the exclusivity we felt
in our accomplishment, as though
the inheritance of our succession
could be more than a two-week administrative
break for the psychologists we
smiled, cried, and screamed
in front of, our fervency kneaded
by time and exposure into marble – cold, glistening
burnished, and plain
                    I was stalled
for hours
            In this, it was a perfect name
a road sign
already rusted, a rail sunken
into grass, a glass pane warped and sinking
onto its frame
                    Dis|ability is
a break, a disavowal
of the norm, a voiceless consonant – a violated
expectation entrenched before intent
and consequence can be
consummated

This alt|erity
between our community and our
minds' shared digression cracked open a
schism
For all of us I knew this was
a space that would grow
And like all
cracks, it was born long before we
saw a need to fill it
But then
I came to appreciate the slowing
force that fissures have on people who
take the ground for granted – a necessary
feature of the larger landscape, an
expression of its stressors, pressures, and
duress otherwise invisible
Cracks and ruptures
speak of incongruous forces
Those visible
in me, those visible in my new friends
those visible in you are a signal of changes necessary
to the landscape around us – far more valuable
than the perceived imperfection
they represent to others

I keep taking
photos of the skies
at dawn

watching the red
crawl forward
reach toward us

as every cloud paints
a different expression
of water
a different
shading
on black canvas
an evolving

habitat
for the approaching
light

Though a similar
red greets
every morning

the frustration
of night's palette is
suddenly evident

– like the sky
we also can't consent

to what is

written over
us

Olive Blue

eyes
are my dad's rarity

two bright circles
resting safe
and undisturbed
around black
an exponential function
of his joy and laughter
infectious happiness
compounded by those creamy
sapphires around pitch
round barriers
bright and full

hint at depth
that by his efforts
I'll never really know

My Father's Eyes

are brown
like my mother's

and I would tell
you more
if pictures and
episodic
memory snapshots
were enough

“Just when I thought I knew relationality,”

another academic said, just before I tuned out
his attempt at an impactful phrasing –
                                        a violated expectation
I didn’t have the patience to hear again
from someone whose understanding
          of relationship
was framed
          limited
by his capacity to
          attend to it

like thinking a single
picture of dawn
can tell you everything
you need to know about the sun

or that sunlight only plays
                                        visibly
          for you

Remi sat
as the dust fell softer
than marine snow
through ocean depths

his brief pause between weavings
lending a kind of substance
to the soup
        thickening
between us

            telling of
my eldest uncle, then a sawyer
who witnessed a bear attack

I learned that bears
will start to consume you
before you die
        your screams
doing little to dissuade them

Sometime later
after my grandfather and others were summoned
Remi told of an entire community
walking the man to an RCMP detachment
        formed in circles
        concentric
with weapons, rifles
        flashlights

while the bear stalked, angry

his meal taken from him

Me wondering
if the bear continued stalking
decades later
anxious to complete the process

Our **Eldest Uncle**

had a hunger
without text
without end

and never enough
witnesses to dismember
his clamorous palate

At his funeral
many relatives
connections long
buried by appetite

arrived
to see that
he
or
the bear
was finally
truly
dead.

The appetite preceded
        and followed him
though it had a different
        shape

Uncle Cecil
had deep
      blue eyes
my first connection
      to him
His eyes were the medium
on which I wrote
our relationship
      unrealized
a massive potential
dreamed until known
          because
for every breath
every sigh
every warning
every tear
every story interrupted by
          children
every unspoken
recollection

I held on to the shared static

      until Remi
could give words
      memories
to them

I think that connections are a line shared
changed with every holder
until they dissipate in the wind
their elements given over
                    to others

Skin is
a binding

a tensile margin
tested
pushed
a singularity
its density
the force of you
and me connecting

its crush
a fabric with
twists and turns
dips and hills
with its twists
dips and scars
where lighter strangulated cells
carry secrets
like soft hairs on the edges of
infinite densities
imperceptible

If I were a universe
each action a galaxy
stretching infinitely

and each thought a gas cloud
waiting to be breathed
used
spent

would my outward growth
contain enough bodies to counter
        my collapse?

Or if there
is a dark centre
a singularity to each of us
that swallows, unsated
        hungrily
our interrupted hopes
barely effected desires

is survival then
a scattering of self?

Falling, I was as brilliant and varied as a universe, but slowly dimming. My trajectory was visible as line on which I keep leaving pieces, bits of myself – to join the shed filaments of long-dead family – wondering how much of myself I would have left. These bits, at first fluid, gathered around the growing string, the tension straightening and hardening, stretching to the point of separation and then stretching further, until their novelty turned memory.

This kept on, my expressions against time lengthening.

Underneath me I could feel there were giants.

I was slowing, but still fell increasingly behind the present, my line unrecognizable to me, but engrossing for others.

Untitled

is a feral invite
to undo

to listen without searching
        for spaces in me to
        fit the words in you

If skin is a translator
between innervation and awareness
transmuting their incompatibility
    piling cells
    over sensations
impossible to outline

anodizing
around this body's
    raw
substrates

    then my voice is fluid
instability compressed
reaching forward
thermalizing

    trailing plasma
magnetic lines unveiling
the direction
my defiance
    took

    a bow shock
its rolling decay
a map for others

I wish I knew these words these pages the way an adult child can know themselves through a found blanket found photo found sibling I wish I knew these words these pages the way a chest-swell and rolling salt-tear on your cheek curls back an ash-fog of forgetting I wish these words these pages were the sting of fresh air after a house fire the flicker vertigo before a coughing fit expelling a somnolent black tar coating and criss-crossed carbon digging in making a home making land anew making black signaling a restart I wrote these words these pages hoping they might skewer meaning through the skin I've grown around this being this roughshod compilation of half-finished limbs each a coping tool no longer used enough to matter I wrote them to brand in return
memories
        the geography of these
        depressions and rises
        too numerous
        to be noticed

a continent of features
crowding the map
appearing banal
from a distance

I wrote them to greet patterns the way a child hopes to meet grandparents they will never know relocating reorienting reviewing photos for missed details inviting a freshness in difference

falling dust in the grip
of the sun's efforts
through the window
translucent like
collagen knots
floating downward
behind pupils

yet through
          everything

Thoughts of mislaid kinships
        absent grandparents
are a dusting on water
a decaying
a laying
of debris that draws fish
and sea mammals
        curious and intelligent
enticed by motes
in a monotony-parched
featureless blue

followed by others
offscourings all

a congress
of the intermittent
        the small

lingering to see
this   dust
        dirt
grow

or fall

shreds
descending

through
the

dark

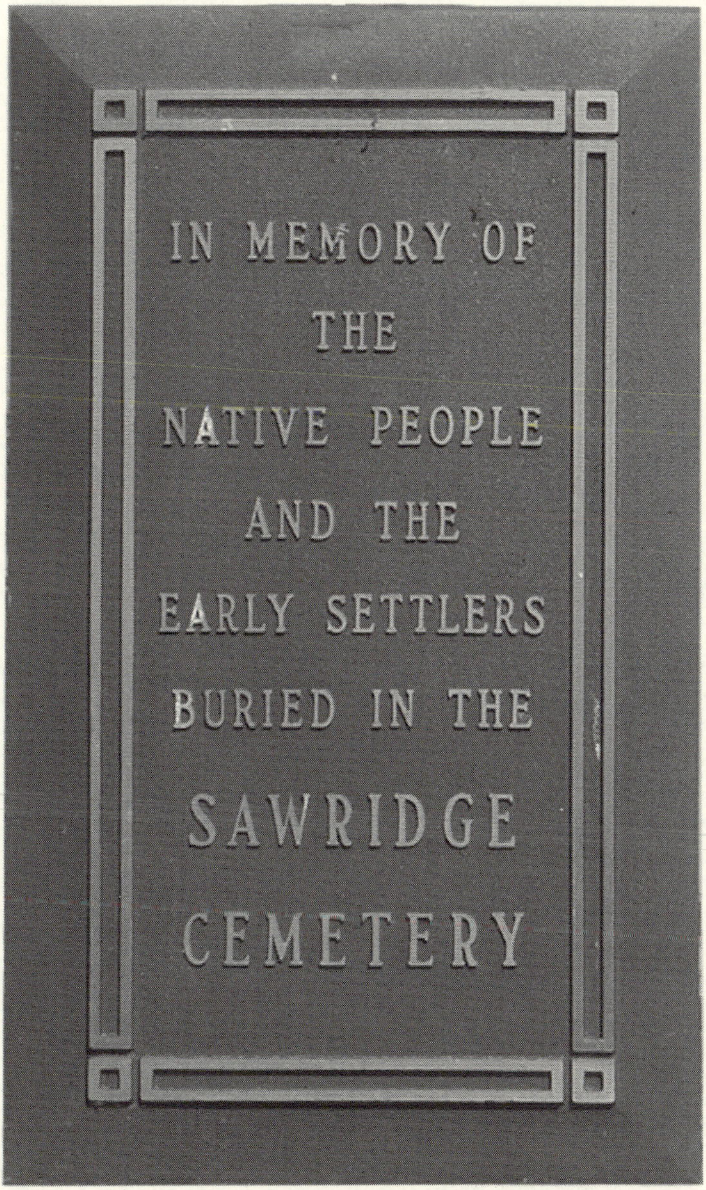
IN MEMORY OF
THE
NATIVE PEOPLE
AND THE
EARLY SETTLERS
BURIED IN THE
SAWRIDGE
CEMETERY

Notes

Page 1: This poem fragment was originally included in my essay "I'm not an expert in intimacy and neither are you," published on the League of Canadian Poets website as part of their National Poetry Month Poetry Pause in 2022.

Page 17: An earlier draft of this poem appeared as "Words" in *Silence to Strength: Writings and Reflections on the Sixties Scoop*, edited by Christine Miskonoodinkwe Smith (Kegedonce Press, 2022).

Page 26: The first lines of this poem reference José Esteban Muńoz's *Cruising Utopia: The Then and There of Queer Futurity*, 10th Anniversary Edition (NYU Press, 2019).

Page 33: An earlier draft of this poem appeared as "Measure" in *Micro-Climate Stories* as part of the *Imagining Climates* project curated by Catherine Bush and Liane Miedema Brown (Guelph Institute for Environmental Research, 2021).

Page 41: The first stanza of this poem references José Esteban Muńoz's *Cruising Utopia: The Then and There of Queer Futurity*, 10th Anniversary Edition (NYU Press, 2019).

Page 49: This poem is in conversation with Joshua Whitehead's essay "Queer Indigenous Futurisms: Stone & Slipstream" presented as part of the Indigenous Literary Studies Association Gathering (Winnipeg, 2024). The roman orthography for the three languages represented here are written in Fiero (Double-Vowel), which is used in Tom Beardy's *Introductory Ojibwe Parts One and Two in Severn Dialect.* This was a core text to Ojibwe learning at the University of Toronto until 2022 and was my introduction to the Algonquian language family (which includes Cree).

Pages 57–58: This poem originally appeared as "Reluctant Superheroes" in *Arc Poetry Magazine, Issue 102: Disability Desirability*, edited by Therese Estacion (Fall 2023).

Page 79: This photo was taken at Sawridge Cemetery, 731C Township Road, Slave Lake, Alberta (copyright Tyler Pennock, edited).

Acknowledgements

The journey that led to this book began in 2004, when the province of Alberta opened its adoption records to adoptees. I owe much to Holly Kramer for her friendship and guidance, and for giving me that copy of Sylvia Van Kirk's *Many Tender Ties* when I was still street-involved, and well before I began reconnecting.

The subsequent discussions that fostered my reconnection to our specific geographies were possible because of the generosity of the biological family members I first reached out to. I owe much to my aunts and uncles for their stories, conversations, and love.

Remy Mailhot shared stories, love, and care in such abundance; many thanks to you, to Myles, and to Keeper!

This book was written with the help of the Indigenous Artist-in-Residence program at Carleton University in the Fall of 2023. Thank you so much to the Department of English Language and Literature, and the Ojigkwanong Indigenous Student Centre for being such kind hosts.

To Dallas Hunt for editing *Skin*, thank you so much for your praise, your insight, your thoughtfulness, your knowledge of our shared territories, and clarity in helping guide these words.

A warm thank you and so much love to Ovila Mailhot for responding to my first Facebook message, and for your *on-point* cover designs!

Orthography for the Cree, Ojicree, and Ojibwe translations of the word for "lake" and the phrase "s/he goes home / returns" were taken from the *itwêwina* Plains Cree Dictionary online, Tom Beardy's Severn Ojibwe series of textbooks, and the University of Minnesota's Ojibwe People's Dictionary, respectively.

This book is for my parents, and the spaces between us that longing made fertile; and most of all for my cousins, who seldom cared for distance in love.

Tyler Pennock, a Two-Spirit adoptee whose Cree and Métis family originates in the Lesser Slave Lake region of Alberta, is a member of Sturgeon Lake Cree Nation (Treaty 8). Their first book, *Bones*, was shortlisted for the Gerald Lampert Memorial Award and the Indigenous Voices Award for Poetry. Their second book, *Blood*, was shortlisted for the 2023 ReLit Poetry award. Tyler began teaching Severn Ojibwe at the Centre for Indigenous Studies at University of Toronto in 2020, where they are now an Assistant Professor, teaching oral tradition and media, as well as contemporary Indigenous history in a Canadian context. Tyler was named the inaugural FASS (Faculty of Arts and Social Sciences) Indigenous Artist-in-Residence at Carleton University in 2023.

MIX
Paper
FSC® C100212

Printed by Imprimerie Gauvin
Gatineau, Québec